Where the Wind Bends Backwards

Erin M. Bertram & Ryan R. Collins

Where the Wind Bends Backwards

Erin M. Bertram & Ryan R. Collins

LeClaire, Iowa

Also by Erin M. Bertram

Memento Mori

Windfall

Inland Sea

The Urge to Believe Is Stronger Than Belief Itself

The Most Wild, Kindly Green

Body of Water

Alluvium

Here, Hunger

Close Your Eyes, Look at Me

Wise Raven

Also by Ryan R. Collins

A New American Field Guide & Song Book

Remote Viewing

Dear Twin Falls

Complicated Weather

Where the Wind Bends Backwards

Erin M. Bertram & Ryan R. Collins

34 pages

Published by 918*studio*

ISBN-10: 0985194464

ISBN-13: 978-0-9851944-6-8

Copyright © 2015 Erin M. Bertram & Ryan R. Collins

Printed in the United States of America

All rights reserved

Cover & interior design by Rivertown Creative & Co.

To St. Louis and Rock Island,
former homes along the river.

Contents

QC (I) 1

STL (I) 2

QC (II) 3

STL (II) 4

QC (III) 5

STL (III) 6

QC (IV) 7

STL (IV) 8

QC (V) 9

STL (V) 10

QC (VI) 11

STL (VI) 12

QC (VII) 13

STL (VII) 14

QC (VIII) 15

STL (VIII) 16

QC (IX) 17

STL (IX) 18

QC (X) 19

STL (X) 20

Acknowledgments 22

QC (I)

We've been called cancer alley but only by people living at high altitudes, where there's less oxygen & a water crisis. Can you imagine living somewhere without water? Lies the thirst doesn't tell. Hurricanes back up the river & slow motion the currents. Locks & damns overwhelmed by the reversal. & the artery blocks, levees a blasphemy against the muddy banks—negative space doesn't save the courtside seats. The playground rims taken down leave rusty backboards & disappointed kids on summer vacation. At some point we stop being encouraged to "get outside," to make something, if only for ourselves, if only once. Compensation's a funny thing—proof of relativity without the radioactivity. You can taste it in the tap water. No more dangerous than smearing your face on the copier glass for a gag at the office—reproduction, facsimile, fax to a bogus number. Rewind the equation & find out what fits on the page. What the record keeps.

STL (I)

These days, things are happening. Often, I leave the apartment by eight, singles crowding my jeans. Often, I'm left balancing. The record shows we've been home to a pair of Great Floods: 1844 & 1993. In 1904, we spread our blankets wide for the World's Fair, where we debuted iced tea & incubators. All year I've had a mean penchant for thick beer & murky water, river stones with ample heft, & a dirty dirty rain. Something to wrap my hands around. Something to send through the mail, flying, over the bridge's rusted edge.

QC (II)

What ever happened to the World's Fairs? Would the internet be filling their voids, multiplying by the day? Some people around here say that we're a Ferris wheel away from being somewhere. I say we're somewhere already & we don't need an amusement park to keep 'em coming, so to speak. We're not Adventureland & the rain here doesn't coagulate overnight. This is a delicate balance. You need wheels to get around here, no pun intended—unless nature intends & then what? Then it's time for wonder, to inspire awe across the tongues of foreign visitors. No more tourist traps until the streets are exhausted from invention. We'll muster an army to sidewalk-chalk the way.

STL (II)

Plaster the streets with epithets, a fistful of words packed with heat lightning & thunder claps of delirium. Pawn tempered responses for a milk crate of wild fire. There are three things you need to survive this weathered bank: a chest packed with rotating seasons, dirt beneath the fingernails, & a change of clothes. When the weatherman predicts rain, you better listen. You better press your good ear to the ground & be ready to weather the ice storm.

QC (III)

We've had enough of pseudoscience to last us several ice ages. The predictions show us clouds on radar, where they are less enjoyable. That which drains the joy from modern life sells us downriver. Short on nothing but compensation: nil times what time's worth equals zero. What in this modern life doesn't equal zero, can't be said in binary code? Plenty, but it's hard to hear with the airshow overhead. They're off! & half in the bag, ready to lower shoulders into the dirt. Ready & doing what needs to be done to stay afloat. It's about time to get trains running & step out from under our cheap umbrellas.

STL (III)

I've had it with hard & fast plans. I've had it with sideburns that curl into my ears like it was somewhere safe to hide. Better to try the backseats of rusted old cars or abandoned warehouses barely standing on the outskirts of town. It's about time we sell ourselves downriver & rotate the laces on our shoes. I'm changing all my strings & playing the same four chords until they ring like a single point of light. Like the ancient choral spheres. I trust my last letter reached you with heady aplomb & scabs on your knees.

QC (IV)

Here we have to make the diving catches. No blood, no foul. Here there are two kinds of people: those that repeat themselves & those that don't. Those that don't generally have musical ability to speak of & holes in their shoes. When they're playing their instruments, you can look thru those holes & see moonlight prism, as though there were nothing strange about any of this. The only strange thing is how electronic devices fail under our touch. Something about the electromagnetic fields associated with our river, bending itself over to deceive any sense of east to west. Those that repeat themselves are generally the suckers, the knee-bleeders, the ones quick to give a tourist directions.

STL (IV)

I am a tourist. I eat food prepared by street vendors & carry maps with me wherever I roam, though I know the value of a ripened peach on a hot to trot August day. When I dérive, I mean it. I talk regularly to strangers on days beginning with T. Confession: I've been found in dried up riverbeds on more than one occasion. Scratch that. I am not a tourist. When I lift my face to the wind, I throw myself wildly at its wide & furrowed brow. When my knapsack weighs down with souvenirs from shinier times, I throw caution & empty bottles to the wind. I scribble postcards. I elucidate. I find myself entraining to the heated breaths of moving trains.

QC (V)

I have the diet of a tourist, but no chasing strumpets around any of these downtowns. Happy hour has nothing to do with days of the week, but does have something to do with conversation. Here everyone talks to strangers. The kids have tasers & know best. *Aquí escribimos mapas con las estrellas*—but there aren't enough translators to go around. The tourists don't seem to mind. The confessional lines are short, mail is forwarded & it's all service with a smile. Still no Amtrak service. The buses stop for waving hands on side streets & stop running when the streetlights come on. No joke—it's the slower pace that keeps 'em coming back, keeps their hands in their pockets. What's translation got to do with that? This is the treaty we make with summer—after, we will set tables & our faces to the hillside.

STL (V)

We're all VIPs out here, with our hands in our pockets & our heads cocked to the crooked sky. An empty ashtray on the balcony, unsent letters clogging the stairwell winding down. This winter could be the one, chakra polishing & falling snow already scrawled in calendar boxes months away. If only August would take its time & hurry up, we'd be on our way to frigid air faster than your friend upriver could knit smoker's gloves from three shades of green. Fact is, however much weight August packs this year, black ice & snow sheets are in the planning stages as we speak. On the mirror above the bathroom sink, toothpaste, toilet paper, these are the days you've been waiting for.

QC (VI)

The provision making goes on & on. Planning too far ahead to see the smoke, so far into the future it sucks out the moment months before it arrives. There's got to be a better way to unlock a cooler & don't forget: we've got one more season before anyone ought to be decking anything. Heat like this knows to do nothing except take the joy out of living, the "out" out of the great outdoors. Satisfying is not a word for this Midwestern climate, but the salty coasts are dissolving, going under & the Great Lakes have 35% of the world's fresh water. Talk about a very important position to be in! But we're leaking out of our pockets & the spillage shows no sign of slowing. It's the goddamned swelter. Hard even for a pillar of Midwestern virtue to hold up the weight of sagging bridge traffic & the coming Fall.

STL (VI)

It is the goddamned swelter. Cowboy boots death for the feet, showers twice daily despite the water waste, the lingering cicadas slow on the drone come nightfall. Come nightfall, I'm even slow on the drone. This is the definition of compression, what it means to press & press a thing until only its core self emerges, baffled, sweating, clumsy on all fours. This pillar of Midwestern virtue's gone slack on us behind our backs, when we'd turned to watch the sun swell & then drop over the mountains' many distinguished brows. There are many faces of desire, each one hot-blooded. Each one bald-faced. Each one plied with fruit bars & visors cocked at audacious angles.

QC (VII)

What bows & bends is hard to forgive. The hard edges of faces beset by the heat soften from the sweating. The sweet waiting that piles upon us while the rain's awaited. Crossed arms & legs only serve to amplify discomfort. Nothing saved by the shade. These boots were made to be not just any pair of shitkickers. They were made to hold up under pressure & duress, the squeeze that results in juice for the people, lemonade stands for the soul. Walking back into climate control, the salt folds outside our souls & brains freeze to the point of brittleness, hollow & icy thin enough to break. We have summer to thank & a lack of eye protection.

STL (VII)

Peeling fingertips is a condition few boast to love. But I say layers lying one on top of another in close quarters provides both comfort & revelation, depending on the angle you peer at it through the beveled parlor window. In my seven window tower, I am painted by the moon in white. There are no pigeons that roost on my sills, though I swear the pin oak, when it waves in the unquiet wind, is itching to get inside my walls. It's true, there's nothing for a broken heart to do save thread the needle & compress the wound, stitch by tiny stitch.

QC (VIII)

Pressure only stops the bleeding. We underuse our fingers & hands enough that the centers of our brains most closely associated with compassion dry up, even as the river floods. The crest getting pushed back by the day & we wait. & you couldn't be more right—it's not just trees trying to get inside. Nature drowns us from the inside out, if we let it. They say the mountains don't care & the river is no different. It's thick but cauterizes no wound & breaks no fall. It's unforgiving to no end. To this end we must recognize & heed the current. Douse the lights & let's get back to the boats. The storm cellars no longer safe & nothing like home.

STL (VIII)

Pressure only stops the bleeding. If you want full out stasis, you're going to have to cauterize, & that could take months. Storm the room staunchly, fill every chair with a healthy sense of impending hurrah! We've grown too old in our weathered jeans for backhanded compliments & blurred edges in the foreground. What's at stake here is not X so much as Y, not saving a few ones at the corner café so much as saving face. In the Land of Evaporating Water, you sip when you sup & never ask for seconds. You command unflinching attention every doorframe, poised, you walk inchoate through.

QC (IX)

Sure the healing goes slow, but the balance is delicate. Like all the rivulet scars across my knuckles, not all the result of violence. Yet that's exactly what spills out of them, ambidextrously. Saving has always been a problem around these parts, since there's no one left to impress, or that's the thinking. The new math tells us to build the lattice high or the vines will choke. What doesn't choke on all the rising murk? We get our fill of bottom-feeding fish & fire. The smoke makes certain after the houses burn down to their doorframes & privacy fences.

STL (IX)

From the balcony, everything is terribly beautiful. Mornings I pull on my boots & make for the third chamber of the café down the street. Dogs on taut leashes follow the scent of my aura & children ask if I'm a monster, to which, once, I replied, Sometimes, & left him blinking, his mother in a fit of muffled laughter. And still I don't know what to make of it but a tall statue of burnished stone somehow suspended, kept in balance by its own weight, against a backdrop of frayed crêpe night. Evenings I fill rooms with frenzied plants, scratch detailed descriptions of dreams across the walls, contemplate the city beneath this city's slumped & crooked streets.

QC (X)

There is no good way to plan a city along a river. The graveyards must be kept above sea level. Everything else is lightning bolts & arrows. Such talk in public causes adults to stare at me like dogs that have just been shown card tricks. Not my line, but trying to figure out which line to follow is like finger-tracing streets on a map of dead-end streets. We go nowhere too often because the people our lines belong to are in their graves. It's hard to hear words as they were first said, unless you put your ear to the river—to hear the bone & silt working their ways.

STL (X)

Eliot said the river is a strong brown god, but eventually the canoe rolls belly up, mouth knotted, gaping, working its slow way down to the bottom, swallowing silt, revising the current along the way. Neither of us is surprised. In a city of flats stacked in rows, leaning against one another hasn't gotten any easier. We find it difficult to talk to strangers despite there being more of them than friends in our periphery. When I pick my way through a crowd of trees to get to the nearest sunspot of crabgrass, the result is clean as math or logic. Beneath the surface, armature. And beneath that, charting its wobble-course, a vault of wrinkled maps, each suspended from festoons. Do you hear the hollersongs of night rubbing its cheek along the length of dawn? Say that you do. Say the river is equal parts folly & fingers worked to the quick. Then barrel crank the hurdy-gurdy of my finely tuned water-heart.

Acknowledgments

We're grateful to the editors of the following publications, in which some of these poems first appeared, at times in different forms:

River Cities' Reader: QC (II)

Sentence: STL (III)
QC (III)
STL (IV)
QC (IV)
STL (V)
QC (V)
STL (VI)
QC (VI)

QC (II) and QC (IV) also previously appeared in the poetry chapbook *Complicated Weather* (Rock Town Press, 2009)

Rockwell

Rockwell is a modern, geometric slab serif. It was
created by Frank Hinman Pierpont. Slab serifs were
created during the industrial revolution to be used
on advertising and billboards. It harkens back to
Mark Twain and posters hung along the river.